CONTENTS

Ireland has a long urban tradition. Dublin, for example, founded in 841, is older than Amsterdam, Berlin, Copenhagen, Helsinki, Madrid, Moscow, Stockholm and many other capital cities of northern Europe. Indeed, the only north European capitals that are significantly older than Dublin are the Roman towns of London, Paris and Vienna.

Fortifications were an essential part of all ancient towns. In medieval art and cartography, defences were perceived as the feature that most characterised a town and made it distinctive from the surrounding countryside. A town wall was not just a security feature, it was also a status symbol, an architectural assertion of the independence of the townspeople and a celebration of their wealth and industry.

The story of fortified towns in Ireland lasts approximately one thousand years, with the year 1700 effectively marking the cut-off point. Prior to 1700, four phases of town development may be distinguished. The first stirrings of town life in Ireland occurred at monasteries during the seventh century, and from about the year 900 we can talk about the existence of monastic towns. The second phase is represented by the Vikings, who established port towns in the ninth and tenth centuries. The third phase occurred during the late twelfth and thirteenth centuries when about fifty new towns were founded under Anglo-Norman patronage. The final phase is expressed by the plantation towns of the sixteenth and seventeenth centuries.

The wars of the seventeenth century ensured that town defences continued to be built and maintained into the 1690s. In 1693, for instance, when the town of Portarlington, Co Laois, was established by a French Huguenot, the Marquis de Ruvigny, defences formed an essential part of the layout. During the eighteenth century, however, town walls were increasingly seen as an encumbrance; narrow gates made it difficult for coach traffic and transport to gain access to the town centre. Gradually, the ditches outside the walls were allowed to silt up and the sites were then sold for building purposes, while the walls themselves were incorporated into new buildings or allowed to decay and collapse.

MONASTIC TOWNS

The first Christian monasteries were established as hermitages by monks who wished to get away from the world and devote themselves to a contemplative life.

5

(Facing page)
Fig 1 *Wall of an
early medieval round
house in the course
of excavation at
Clonmacnoise,
Co Offaly.*

From an early date, however, these centres came to be regarded as refuges and places of sanctuary, attracting not only the sick and the poor but, by the late seventh century, a mixed population of criminals and offenders, all of whom began to settle within or beside the monasteries. The canonical legislation of the early eighth century speaks disparagingly of those monasteries that permitted murderers, thieves, adulterers, perjurers, traders, jesters and prostitutes within their bounds. In the eyes of the canon lawyers, it was improper for abbots to allow holy places to be soiled by such persons, and their solution was to restrict access by dividing the site into areas of sanctuary, called *sanctus* (holy), *sanctior* (holier) and *sanctissimus* (holiest). The most sacred area, consisting of the church, shrines and monastic burial ground, was located at the core, and, in theory, only men and women vowed to the religious life were admitted to this sector. In the middle ground, according to the laws, 'into its streets the crowds of common people not much given to wickedness, are allowed to enter', while the outermost area was one into which 'men who had been guilty of homicide, adulterers and prostitutes, with permission and according to custom, are allowed to enter'.

One effect of this reorganisation was that craftworking and trade developed in the middle and outer sectors of the monastery. At Clonmacnoise, Co Offaly, archaeological excavations have located a domestic area outside the centrally placed ecclesiastical zone (Fig 1). The remains consist of round houses, boundary fences, a boat slip, and paved surfaces, as well as evidence for a range of craftworking activities, including bronzeworking, goldworking, ironworking, jet bracelet manufacture and combmaking, all in contexts predominantly of seventh and eighth-century date.

Enclosure was an important aspect of every monastery and some monastic rules imposed a penance on anyone who went outside the enclosure without permission. Early accounts indicate that the monastery was bounded by a rampart high enough to prevent the monks from seeing out and so encouraging them to concentrate on heavenly matters. The growth of warfare between monasteries during the eighth century, and their increasing use in times of attack as places of refuge, both for people and livestock, indicates that enclosures were also needed for security. By the tenth and eleventh centuries, and perhaps even before, the earthworks enclosing the larger monasteries such as Sierkieran, Co Offaly, and Downpatrick, Co Down, were comparable in scale to the town defences of Dublin. It is not

surprising, therefore, to find that in 1103 the monastic town of Armagh resisted a siege by the army of Muirchertach Ua Briain, king of Munster.

The surviving earthworks at early ecclesiastical sites are generally comparable with those encompassing secular ringforts and show a similar variety in scale and mode of construction. They normally consist of earthen banks with external ditches and, as with secular sites, the more powerful and wealthy the monastery, the stronger and larger was its enclosure. The surviving remains at Sierkieran, said to have been built in 927 by the high king Donnchadh mac Flann Sinna, enclose an area of approximately 12 hectares and consist of two coterminous banks and ditches. The banks vary between 7m and 10m in width and survive to a height of 2m, while the ditches are 3m deep in places. Excavations at Kilpatrick, Co Westmeath, revealed that the ditch was cut into bedrock to a depth of 3m and was almost 6m wide. The original height of these ramparts is difficult to gauge, but the surviving wall height of 6m at Inishmurray, Co Sligo, provides some indication of what was regarded as a desirable height. Entry to the enclosure was by means of a gateway, again probably comparable to those found in secular contexts. The most elaborate surviving example is the twelfth-century gatehouse at Glendalough, Co Wicklow, which had an upper storey and may have been fortified.

Armagh provides us with the best glimpse of what one of these monastic towns looked like (Fig 2). Founded by St Patrick, it has been the ecclesiastical capital of Ireland since the seventh century. The monastery was built on a prominent hill, whose summit is a terrace about 250m across. This is known in numerous annals of the ninth to twelfth centuries as 'the Rath', a name which suggests that it was enclosed by a palisaded earthwork. The gate of this enclosure is mentioned on several occasions and within it were the principal ecclesiastical buildings. These comprised the *damhliac mór* (the principal church), two churches known as *damhliac an tsabhaill* and *damhliac na toe*, the Céli Dé priory (established before 919), the Library, the abbot's house, a grove, a cemetery, and at least one round tower. The area outside this enclosure was divided into three precincts, known as trians. The *trian saxan* ('English precinct') was located to the north and north-east, where English Street still preserves its name. The *trian masain* ('middle precinct') lay on the south-east, and the *trian mór* ('large precinct') on the west. Annalistic references of 1112, 1121 and 1166 indicate that these trians contained streets and houses, which were lived in by students, craftworkers and functionaries. Outside,

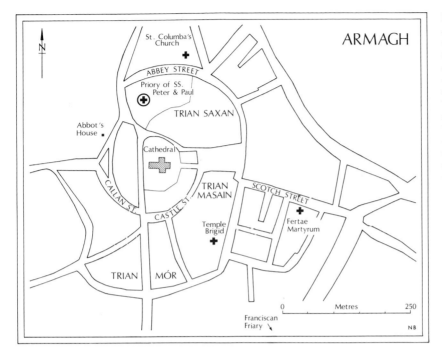

Fig 2 *Plan of Armagh. The position of the inner enclosure ('the rath') is indicated by Callan Street and Castle Street. The* trians *were located within the outer enclosure, which is marked by the streets curving south from Abbey Street. The* trian mór *appears to have continued west of the town.*

to the east, there was a suburb around the old cemetery known as Fertae Martyrum, where excavations have recovered the workshop evidence of a lignite jeweller, dating to the tenth/eleventh centuries.

Both documentary and archaeological records show that the origins of monastic towns lie in the seventh century, but the evidence for trade and exchange increases substantially after the year 900. Markets and fairs were held where goods could be purchased or exchanged. Kings began to build their palaces at or beside churches: the O'Briens at Killaloe, Co Clare, the O'Conors at Tuam, Co Galway, and the MacMurroughs at Ferns, Co Wexford. There is also increasing documentary evidence for domestic structures. Records show that twenty houses were burned at Armagh in 1116; between seventy and eighty houses were destroyed at Duleek, Co Meath, in 1123; eighty houses were demolished during rebuilding work at Derry in 1162, while 105 houses are referred to at Clonmacnoise in 1179. All of these developments were spurred on by the arrival of the Vikings and the foundation of a series of port towns which functioned as windows on Europe and the avenues through which continental developments reached the interior of Ireland.

9

VIKING TOWNS

The first recorded Viking raid on Ireland occurred in 795, but it was not until the middle of the ninth century that the Scandinavians began to establish settlements. Dublin and Annagassan, Co Louth, the earliest of these, were founded in 841, but the physical form of both settlements is unclear. The term used to describe them in the annalistic entries is *longphort*, a word that indicates a fortress or enclosure associated with ships. In 914 a great fleet of Scandinavians landed at Waterford, initiating a major phase of urbanisation. Cork was probably established in the following year, Dublin was refounded in 917, and Limerick in 922. Wexford was probably established at this time also, but the first documentary reference to a settlement there does not occur until 935.

Dublin

Archaeological excavation in Dublin has shed a great deal of light on the nature of these tenth-century towns. Dublin was located on a spur overlooking the confluence of the rivers Liffey and Poddle in the vicinity of the present-day Christ Church Cathedral. Its dominant topographical feature was a long narrow ridge running parallel to the river. The location was easy to defend, but the new site also had a number of other advantages. It had a sheltered haven at a point where the Liffey was not only broad but fordable; it was at the intersection of three major long-distance land routes, and it was close to Dublin Bay.

The initial town (Fig 3) was established around the crossroads formed by the intersection of Castle Street, Christ Church Place (the former Skinner's Row), Fishamble Street and Werburgh Street. Archaeological excavation has revealed that the town was divided into a series of long narrow properties, with houses fronting onto the streets, and it was enclosed by an earthen bank from *c*925. About the year 1000, or shortly afterwards, this area was extended westwards so as to include High Street and Nicholas Street. The area, comprising approximately twelve hectares, was enclosed by a stone wall commenced *c*1100 and finished *c*1130. By the twelfth century, however, suburbs had been established on the north side of the river, around St Michan's Church, to the east in Dame Street and to the south around the churches of St Bride, St Kevin and St Patrick.

Within the town, virtually all of the buildings were of wood, mostly ash. Post-

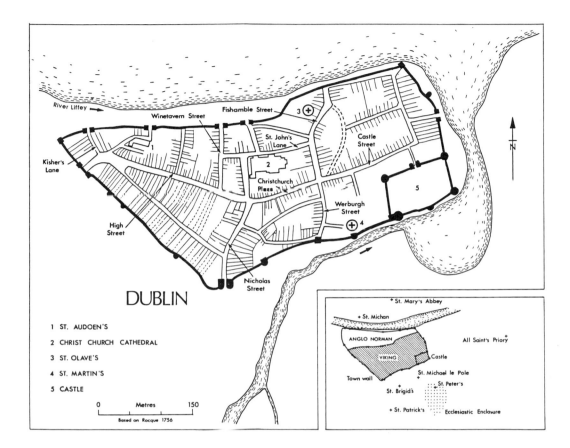

DUBLIN

1 ST. AUDOEN'S

2 CHRIST CHURCH CATHEDRAL

3 ST. OLAVE'S

4 ST. MARTIN'S

5 CASTLE

0   Metres   150

Based on Rocque 1756

and-wattle was the most common construction, with the walls composed of upright hammer-driven circular posts and horizontal layers of wattles or rods woven between them in basketry fashion. In many houses a double row of post-and-wattle was present, suggesting that the space in between may have been insulated. The buildings tend to be rectangular in plan, many appear to have been hip-roofed, and nearly all must have been thatched.

Recent research on the houses of Viking Dublin has identified five major building types. A typical house measured about 8.5m by 4.5m, with a wall 1.25m high. The roof was supported on four main posts arranged in a rectangle within the floor area. The door was located in the end wall and its stout jambs appear to have played a part in supporting the roof. The floor space was sub-divided into three,

Fig 3 *Plan of Dublin in the Late Viking Age. The exact number of towers and gates on the Viking town wall is not known and the diagram shows their position in the late Middle Ages. Dublin Castle, commenced in 1204, may have been on the site of an earlier Viking fort.*

11

with the central strip, sometimes paved or gravelled, being the broadest. A rectangular stone-kerbed fireplace was located in the centre. Along the side walls, two raised areas of turves and brushwood formed benches, which also served as beds. Sometimes corner areas near the doorways were partitioned off and provided with a separate entrance for greater privacy. The floor was covered with a layer of vegetation of a texture akin to mouldy hay, and analysis indicates that flies, fleas and mites were present in abundance.

There is considerable evidence for tradespeople and craftwork. The range of artisans included carpenters, coopers, turners, shipwrights, carvers, blacksmiths, silversmiths, goldsmiths, bronzesmiths, leadsmiths, combmakers, weavers and pewterers. Some of their workshops have been discovered: a bronze pin-manufacturer at High Street, combmakers at High Street and Christ Church Place, amber jewellers at High Street and Fishamble Street. In the eleventh and twelfth centuries, Dublin was the home of a particularly skilful group of carvers and bronzeworkers who produced some remarkably accomplished works of art. Trade was also an important aspect of town life. Balance scales, ingots of gold and silver and large quantities of coins point to the importance of the merchants who traded with England, especially the Chester area, and with the north-west of France. The presence of Walrus ivory, soapstone vessels and amber indicates that trade was maintained with Scandinavia, while the discovery of silk shows that the trading network stretched further to the east. Trade within Ireland is evidenced by the presence of souterrain ware, suggesting contact with Ulster. From its Irish hinterland, also, the town obtained the wool, hides and slaves that formed Dublin's major exports.

Waterford

Waterford was established on a prominent peninsular ridge overlooking the confluence of the Suir and St John's River, which was easily defended on the landward side, where there was only one approach route (Fig 4). Like Dublin, the town seems to have expanded westwards from a fortified area around Reginald's Tower in the course of the tenth and eleventh centuries. High Street and Peter Street appear to have been the major streets and the layout of the town has a rectilinear plan.

12

The archaeological evidence from Waterford dates to the eleventh and twelfth

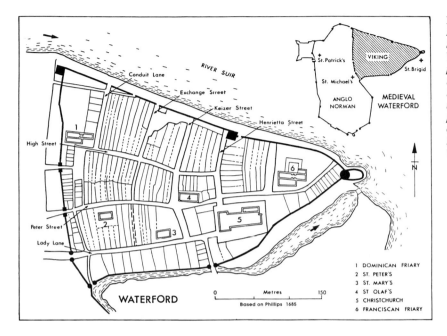

Fig 4 *Plan of Hiberno-Scandinavian Waterford. The street pattern, churches and town defences are based on Phillips' map of 1685. The plot pattern is that of c1840, but it may have originated in Viking times.*

centuries, but it parallels the Dublin record in many ways. About one hundred buildings are known and, like Dublin, most of the houses were contiguously arranged and fronted onto the streets. There are, however, some instances of houses at the centre of blocks of land, with no apparent access by pathway or street, as well as sunken-featured buildings, reflecting Anglo-Saxon influence. About 35m of the eleventh-century earthen defences have been excavated. The bank was 4m wide at the base and originally it was probably about 3m high. Outside the bank was a ditch, 8m wide at the top and varying between 2m and 2.5m in depth. In the second quarter of the twelfth century, the bank was demolished and the ditch was backfilled to accommodate a substantial stone wall. No trace of the earthen defences was found on the south, where the marshy ground and St John's River presumably afforded sufficient defence. Evidence for a pre-Norman gateway, 1.72m wide, was found in Peter Street.

Apart from Christ Church Cathedral, two other churches are known to have existed within Viking Age Waterford: St Peter's, where archaeological excavations uncovered the foundations of an apsidal Romanesque church in 1987, and the church of St Olaf, whose cult in Ireland is exclusively Scandinavian. The presence

13

of dedications outside the walled area to Saints Brigid, Michael and Patrick, who are frequently associated with pre-Norman dedications, may indicate that some form of suburb existed by the twelfth century. In this regard, the discovery of house foundations built in the twelfth-century fill of the fosse at Lady Lane suggests that there was already pressure on building space within the town by this time.

Other Viking settlements

At Cork, the Scandinavians established themselves on an island in the estuary of the river Lee, just below the monastery dedicated to St Finbar or Bairre. Like Dublin, the site was easy to defend and it provided ready access to the sea. By the twelfth century it was defended by a stone wall with gates, and there was an unenclosed suburb on the south bank of the river between South Gate Bridge, first referred to in 1163, and the monastery. In Limerick, archaeological excavations have uncovered three sunken-floored buildings, apparently of twelfth-century date, and a section of the town defences. The latter consisted of a clay bank 10m long and 1.7m high which was revetted by a stone wall. Two house plots have been excavated in Bride Street, Wexford; occupation commenced in that part of the town shortly after the year 1000.

By the middle of the twelfth century the Irish urban network consisted of five port towns and about fifteen monastic towns. With the coming of the Anglo-Normans, however, this network was totally transformed.

ANGLO-NORMAN TOWNS

The initial impact of Anglo-Norman society on Ireland is conventionally dated to 1169, but archaeological research has shown that the invasion was simply the culmination of a long period of acculturation. By 1176, the process of establishing a manorial society similar to that which existed in Britain and on the Continent was well under way. In this society, in which land and lordship were of central importance, towns played an essential role. They functioned primarily as market places for the produce of the manor and the surrounding countryside, but they were also centres in which imported commodities, such as wine, salt and fine silks, could be obtained, and they were the homes of specialist craftworkers. The town

provided the lord of the manor with annual rents, and in times of war the loyalty of
the townspeople could be relied upon.

The initial urban activity of the Anglo-Normans consisted of expanding pre-
existing towns such as Dublin, Kilkenny, and Kells, Co Meath. New towns, like
Drogheda, Co Louth, were founded before the end of the twelfth century,
however, and they were a popular feature of the thirteenth century. The
distribution of these towns is predominantly eastern, based on a line connecting
Waterford with Dundalk and having linear extensions westwards to Dingle, Co
Kerry, Galway and Sligo, and a coastal spread northwards as far as Coleraine, Co
Derry. Large parts of Ireland were unaffected by towns, including northern and
central Ulster, as well as areas of Connacht, Cork-Kerry, Laois-Offaly and
Wicklow, simply because the Anglo-Normans never penetrated these areas. The
chronology of town foundation is relatively short, with Roscommon, established
in 1282, as the latest example.

Town defences

A characteristic of Anglo-Norman towns was the presence of defences, but not all
towns had walls of stone. Earthen ramparts, such as those which protected
Duleek, Co Meath, or formed the earliest defences of Drogheda, could withstand
attack every bit as successfully as walls of stone. The possession of a stone wall,
however, marked a certain coming of age: it announced to all and sundry that you
had arrived at a town that held its urban status in high regard. The town walls of
medieval Ireland were relatively straightforward affairs. They consisted
predominantly of a curtain wall, with as few mural towers and gatehouses as
possible (Fig 5; Pls 1, 2). Only in Dublin and the wealthier port towns, such as
Waterford and Cork, were non-essential mural towers to be found, and these
functioned primarily as residences (Figs 6, 7; Pls 3, 4). The curtain wall itself was
plain and tended to be protected by a battlemented walkway; arrowloops and
embrasures at ground level, like those that survive at Kilkenny, were relatively
few. The majority of urban gatehouses were rectangular buildings (Fig 8), such as
those still standing at Athenry (Pl 5) and Loughrea, Co Galway, Carlingford, Co
Louth and Kilmallock, Co Limerick (Fig 9; Pls 6, 7). In the larger towns, more
elaborate twin-towered structures were sometimes built, like the barbican of St
Laurence's Gate in Drogheda.

15

cont. p 31

Fig 5 *The town wall of Fethard, Co Tipperary, in the course of renovation. The main part of the curtain wall is of thirteenth/fourteenth-century date, while both the mural tower and the tower of the parish church behind were built during the fifteenth and sixteenth centuries.*

Fig 6 *Medieval mural tower at Kells, Co Meath.*

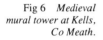

16

Pl 1 *Fifteenth-century mural towers at Kells, Co Kilkenny, a settlement that was abandoned after the Reformation when the Augustinian Priory on which it depended was dissolved.*

Pl 2 *A stretch of the curtain wall and a mural tower at the deserted town of Rindown, Co Roscommon.*

17

(Facing page)
Pl 3 *Reginald's Tower, Waterford, built in the thirteenth century on the site of the former Viking fortress of Dundory.*

Pl 4 *Mural tower of thirteenth/fourteenth-century date, Athenry, Co Galway.*

Pl 5 *The fifteenth-century North Gate at Athenry, Co Galway, after renovation work in 1979.*

19

Pl 6 *The east gate of the shrunken medieval town founded beside the Benedictine Priory at Fore, Co Westmeath.*

Pl 7 *'King's Castle', a gatehouse of fifteenth/sixteenth-century date at Kilmallock, Co Limerick. The pointed windows were inserted in the late eighteenth century.*

20

Pl 8   *The remains of
the fifteenth-century
market cross at
Athenry, Co Galway.*

21

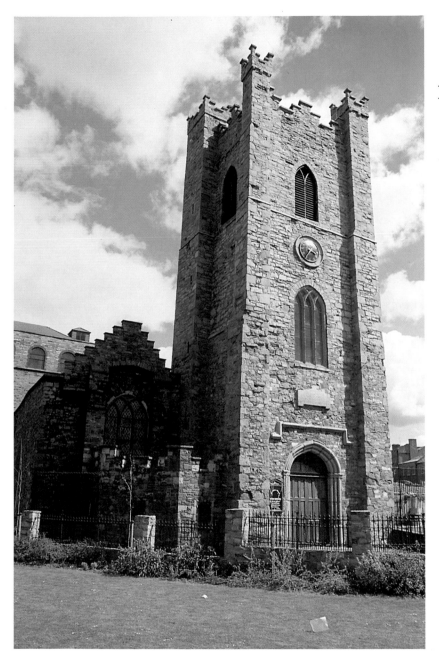

(Facing page)
Pl 9   *St Leger's Castle, Ardee, Co Louth, the largest example of a fifteenth-century fortified town house in Ireland.*

Pl 10   *The medieval tower of St Audeon's parish church, Dublin.*

23

Pl 11 *The Bridge Castle, Athy, Co Kildare, probably the 'new tower built on the bridge' in 1417. An extension was added to the left of the original tower in the nineteenth century.*

Pl 12 *Limerick Castle dominated the western approach to the town and was located, in common with most other Anglo-Norman castles, on the edge of the town.*

Pl 13   *The thirteenth-century cathedral of St Canice, Kilkenny, with its pre-Norman round tower.*

Pl 14   *High Street, Kilkenny, with the Tholsel projecting into the street at the point where the medieval market stalls would have been concentrated.*

Pl 15 *The fourteenth-century Lady Chapel of St John's Augustinian Priory, Kilkenny, was transformed into a parish church in the nineteenth century.*

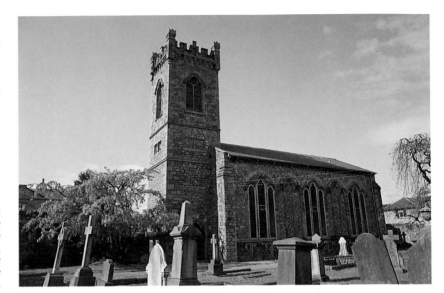

Pl 16 *The thirteenth-century Dominican Friary ('Black Abbey'), Kilkenny, which was located outside the town defences.*

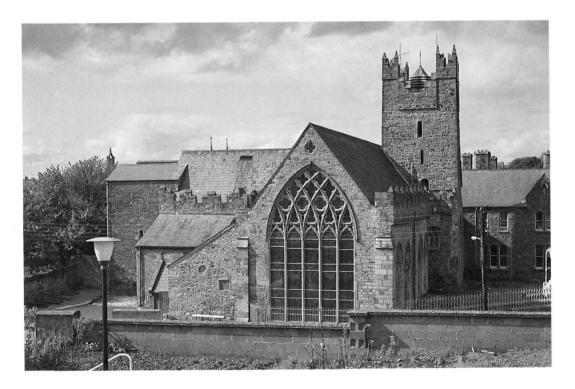

Pl 17 Rothe House, Kilkenny, the residence of a wealthy merchant, was built in 1594.

Pl 18 Remains of sixteenth- and seventeenth-century houses preserved behind modern façades in Parliament Street, Kilkenny.

27

Pl 19 *Shee Alms House, Kilkenny, built to accommodate twelve poor people in 1582.*

28

Fig 7 *Medieval mural tower at Waterford.*

NORTH ELEVATION

SECTION

WALL WALK

WALL WALK

BATTER

BATTER UNDER GROUND LEVEL

COLLAPSED STONES

COLLAPSED STONES

PLAN

0 Metres 3

RECONSTRUCTION

RINDOWN : GATEHOUSE

Fig 8 *Ground plan, elevation and conjectural reconstruction of the thirteenth-century gatehouse at the deserted town of Rindown, Co Roscommon.*

29

Fig 9 *Blossom's*
Gate, Kilmallock,
Co Limerick, a
fifteenth-century
gatehouse with a
partly modernised
gateway.

cont. from p 15

The gatehouses permitted control over individuals entering and leaving the town. Spies and suspected criminals might be arrested and diseased persons kept out, but the primary function of the gatehouse was as a customs post. Tolls had to be paid on all commodities brought into the town for sale. The monies so collected were meant to be expended on public works, on the repair and maintenance of the town wall, on building bridges and on paving the streets. In practice, however, the mechanism of collecting tolls was so cumbersome that it allowed plenty of room for embezzlement, and by the year 1400 most Irish towns had discovered that it was cheaper to contract out the collection of tolls. 'Farming the murage', as this practice came to be known, proved to be long-lived. In 1835 the Municipal Corporations Commissioners, appointed to investigate and reform parliamentary boroughs, were surprised to discover that murage was still being collected for the maintenance of walls which had long since ceased to exist. For most small market towns, however, it remained one of the few sources of steady income, and at Cashel, Co Tipperary, for instance, murage was still collected at markets and fairs until the 1950s.

Town layout

The street layout of the Anglo-Norman towns in Ireland was predominantly linear, consisting, like Fethard, Co Tipperary, of a long main street (Fig 10). More complex layouts with chequer plans, like Drogheda, New Ross, Co Wexford, and Galway, also occur (Fig 11). The marketplace was located in the main street of the linear towns and was occasionally embellished with a market cross. Sometimes the market cross was of wood, as at Ardee, Co Louth, but more usually it was of stone and mounted on steps. The only example surviving *in situ* is at Athenry, Co Galway; it is of pillar type and dates to the fifteenth century (Fig 12; Pl 8).

The colonists who settled in the original Anglo-Norman towns were given a plot of land on which to build a house for themselves and their family. In the smaller market towns this normally stretched back from the main street to the town wall. It was termed a burgage plot and the people who took up these plots were known as burgesses. The plots tended to be much longer than they were broad, and accordingly it was normal to place the short or gable end of the house on the street frontage. Behind the house there might be subsidiary buildings, sheds, cess pits, wells and a garden in which herbs, vegetables or fruit might be grown. Tower *31*

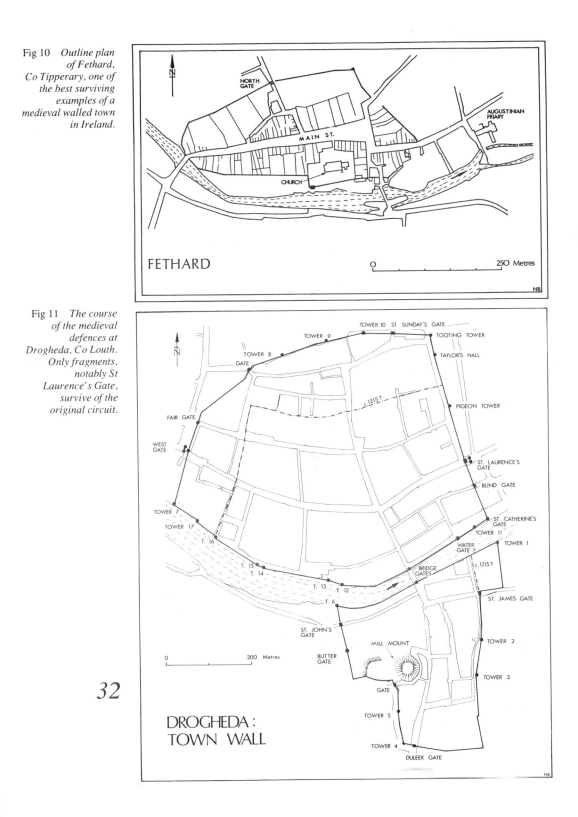

Fig 10 *Outline plan
of Fethard,
Co Tipperary, one of
the best surviving
examples of a
medieval walled town
in Ireland.*

Fig 11 *The course
of the medieval
defences at
Drogheda, Co Louth.
Only fragments,
notably St
Laurence's Gate,
survive of the
original circuit.*

32

houses began to appear in towns during the fourteenth century and they became a feature of Irish towns in the fifteenth and sixteenth centuries. There are good surviving examples at Ardee, Carlingford, Cashel, Co Tipperary, Fethard, Limerick and Kinsale, Co Cork (Figs 13, 14; Pl 9).

The majority of dwellings, however, would have been timber-built and thatched, although a percentage would have been roofed with shingles or slates. Archaeologically, very little is known about the nature of these timber buildings. At Wexford, post-and-wattle houses of Viking Age type were still being constructed during the thirteenth century, but it is not known if the practice continued later than this time.

In towns such as Carrickfergus, Co Antrim, Elizabethan maps depict simple mud-walled houses plastered externally. Timber-framed houses were almost

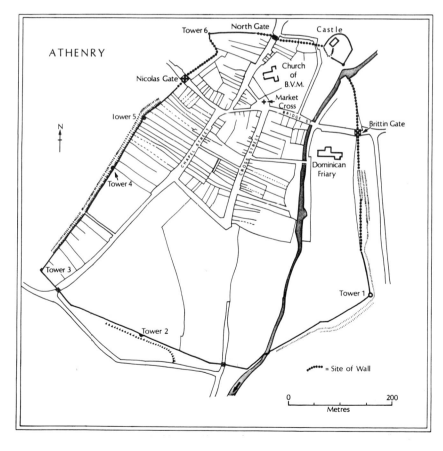

Fig 12   *Outline plan of Athenry, Co Galway. The town has the longest circuit of surviving medieval town walls in Ireland.*

33

Fig 13 *Late medieval fortified tower house known as Taaffe's Castle, Carlingford, Co Louth. The castellated building on the right was added in the seventeenth century.*

Fig 14 *Plans and elevations of the late medieval tower house known as 'the mint', Carlingford, Co Louth.*

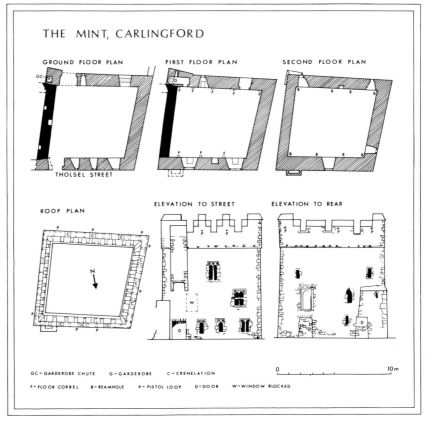

THE MINT, CARLINGFORD

GROUND FLOOR PLAN   FIRST FLOOR PLAN   SECOND FLOOR PLAN

THOLSEL STREET

ROOF PLAN   ELEVATION TO STREET   ELEVATION TO REAR

GC – GARDEROBE CHUTE   G – GARDEROBE   C – CRENELATION

F – FLOOR CORBEL   B – BEAMHOLE   P – PISTOL LOOP   D – DOOR   W – WINDOW BLOCKED

0   10 m

34

certainly the dominant house type until they began to be replaced with stone buildings during the sixteenth century. The many documentary references to 'timber houses' should probably be understood as referring to timber-framed buildings, but the only examples whose layout can be determined are confined to Dublin and Drogheda. The walls of most timber-framed buildings were constructed of post-and-wattle plastered externally. Internally, one can only assume that some of these walls were panelled to keep the damp and cold at bay.

In many houses, the ground floor on the street frontage functioned as a shop where the owner's craftwork was exposed for sale. Lean-to stalls might be set up on market day, but most shops tended to be small booth-like affairs. This is the explanation for the medieval name Bothe (Booth) Street which occurred in a number of towns, including Drogheda, where it is now known by the grander-sounding name of Shop Street. Arcaded walkways, which are a feature of many English and continental towns, developed at Kilkenny, where the arcade at Rothe House, built in 1594, is perhaps the best surviving example.

Trade and commerce

Urban Anglo-Norman society consisted essentially of merchants, craftworkers and labourers. By the fifteenth century the merchant class had obtained a firm grip on the government of most Irish towns and in effect formed an oligarchy. Most craftwork was home-based and family-oriented. The range of urban craftworkers included carpenters, coopers, drapers, embroiderers, glovers, hosiers, furriers, potters, shoemakers, smiths, tailors and weavers. Related to these were the food providers: bakers, butchers, fishmongers, grocers, poulterers and vintners. In the larger towns there is evidence for the concentration of craftworkers in certain streets and areas. Names like Broguemaker's Hill in Kilkenny, Skinner's Row in Dublin and Dyer Street in Drogheda indicate the former quarters of leather and textile workers. Some trades had to be conducted outside the town, particularly those utilising ovens or kilns that might explode, with the consequent risk of setting fire to the town. In Dublin, for instance, both Cook Street and Crocker Street are found outside the old (Scandinavian) walled town, while the pottery kilns discovered at Carrickfergus, Co Antrim, and Downpatrick, Co Down, were also located outside the built-up areas of the town.

The general merchant was an individual about whom there is little information *35* until the sixteenth century. Some, like Germyn Lynch of Galway, were entrepreneurs who sailed ships to France and Spain, bringing pilgrims to the shrine of St James at Compostella and returning with French and Spanish wines. Others would simply have been dependent on suppliers from the larger port towns. The port areas of Dublin and Drogheda have been investigated archaeologically and the docksides were found to be front-braced, ie supported from the front rather than from behind, in common with the tradition of Atlantic Europe. Some towns, such as Dublin and Tralee, Co Kerry, had shallow harbours, which meant that large vessels had to anchor in the bay and offload their cargoes into smaller boats. It was because of Dublin's shallow harbour that Dalkey developed in the fourteenth and fifteenth centuries into the port of Dublin. In other cases, such as Clonmines and Bannow, Co Wexford, the silting up of the harbour led to the eventual abandonment of the town. In some instances the town wall directly overlooked the dockside, but this could be an obstacle to commerce, and in other places it seems that warehouses fronted directly onto the quayside.

Churches

The Church was omnipresent in medieval society. Architecturally its towers and spires dominated the skyline and it was frequently the meeting-place of the corporation and guilds (Figs 15, 16; Pl 10). A characteristic feature of the Anglo-Norman town is that it possessed just one parish church. Monasteries, run by religious orders, were also a feature. Contemplative orders, such as the Cistercians at St Mary's in Dublin or the Benedictines at Cashel, were a rarity, and in general the religious orders represented in the towns can be divided into mendicants and hospitallers. The mendicants included the Augustinians, Carmelites, Dominicans and Franciscans, and their friaries were almost always built outside the town wall or on the perimeter edge. A hospital was a regular feature of every medieval Irish town and was generally maintained by an order such as the Fratres Cruciferi. These hospitals catered for the aged, sick and infirm townspeople, and because of the dangers of contagious diseases they were usually built some distance from the town, perhaps a mile or so. The remains of very few medieval hospitals survive, but their location is frequently preserved in placenames such as Spiddal, Spittleland, Maudlin or Maudlinland.

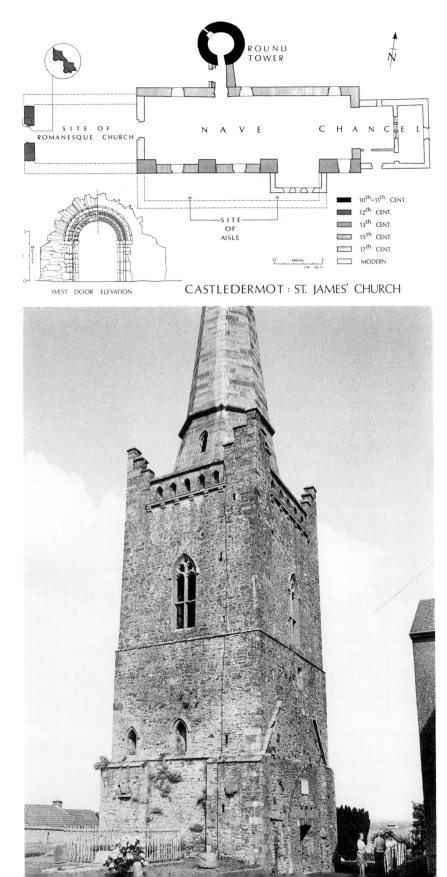

Fig 15 *Ground plan of a typical urban parish church showing many phases of building and rebuilding at Castledermot, Co Kildare.*

ROUND TOWER

N

SITE OF ROMANESQUE CHURCH

N A V E   C H A N C E L

■ 10ᵗʰ–11ᵗʰ CENT.
▨ 12ᵗʰ CENT.
▨ 13ᵗʰ CENT.
▨ 15ᵗʰ CENT.
▨ 17ᵗʰ CENT.
□ MODERN

SITE OF AISLE

0   Metres   5
   J W delt

WEST DOOR ELEVATION

CASTLEDERMOT : ST. JAMES' CHURCH

Fig 16 *The fifteenth-century tower of St Columba's parish church, Kells, Co Meath. The steeple was added in 1783.*

37

Castles

If the Church presided over the spiritual welfare of the townspeople, it was the castle that dominated their political life. Virtually all Anglo-Norman towns in Ireland were developments from the manor and there were very few towns, like New Ross, which did not have a seigneurial castle either in the town, as at Dublin, or immediately outside it, as at Ardee, Co Louth and Buttevant, Co Cork. Generally the castle tended to be located in an angle of the town walls, as at Athenry, Co Galway and Trim, Co Meath, where it could be easily protected, not just from outside attack but also from the townspeople themselves in the event of rebellion (Figs 17, 18; Pl 12).

Fig 17 *Outline plan of Trim, Co Meath. Note the position of the castle on the edge of the town.*

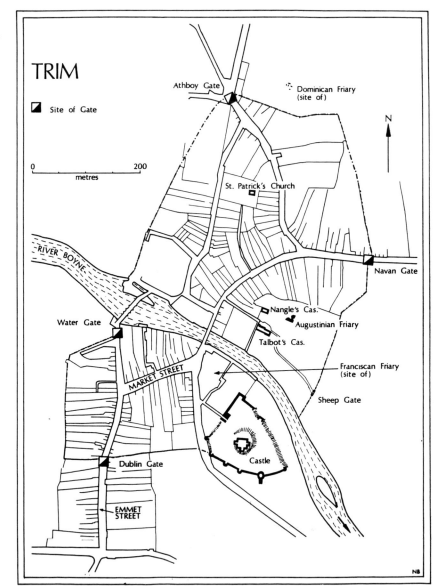

38

Kilkenny — a typical medieval town

The general pattern of development of medieval Irish towns is one of expansion in the thirteenth century, contraction in the fourteenth, consolidation in the fifteenth century and expansion again in the sixteenth. A typical example of this pattern is provided by Kilkenny, which even before the coming of the Normans was an important ecclesiastical site, an episcopal see, and an administrative centre for the kings of Ossory. The Anglo-Normans established a borough here by 1176, but it was not until the early years of the thirteenth century that the settlement began to expand. Throughout the Middle Ages, and indeed until 1843, the town was divided administratively into two sections: the Irishtown based on St Canice's Cathedral (Pl 13), and the Hightown or Englishtown.

Fig 18 *Aerial view of Trim, Co Meath, with the tower of the Augustinian Priory ('Yellow Steeple') on the north side of the river. On the right is the medieval Sheep Gate.*

39

The ecclesiastical site was the focus that attracted the initial Anglo-Normans to Kilkenny, and when Stanihurst wrote his *Chronicles of Ireland* (1577), the Irishtown proudly claimed to be the older of the two settlements. A handful of documents survive relating to the growth of the Hightown, whose development occurred in four stages (Fig 19; Pl 14). The castle, founded before 1192, was the

Fig 19   *Outline plan of medieval Kilkenny.*

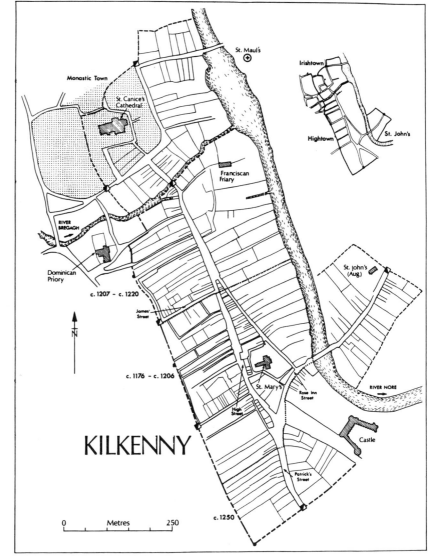

St. Maul's

Monastic Town

Irishtown

St. Canice's Cathedral

Hightown

St. John's

Franciscan Friary

RIVER BREGAGH

St. John's (Aug)

Dominican Priory

c. 1207 – c. 1220

James' Street

c. 1176 – c. 1206

RIVER NORE

St. Mary's

Rose Inn Street

High Street

KILKENNY

Castle

Patrick's Street

0   Metres   250

c. 1250

focus for the initial settlement, which was delimited by the parish boundary of St Mary's on the south and James's Street on the north. The second stage of growth occurred c1207 with the grant by the bishop to William Marshall, lord of Leinster, of land to enlarge the town between James's Street and the river Bregagh. The third stage was the addition of the land between the parish boundary of St Mary's and the late thirteenth-century wall, on the south. The fourth unit lay on the east bank of the river Nore, where settlement was initiated shortly after 1200, when the Augustinian priory of St John was founded (Pl 15). The foundation of the Dominican Friary (c1225) west of the town may indicate the existence of a suburb in that area (Pl 16), and other suburbs are known to have existed south of the town in Patrick Street and Archer Street (Flemingstown). In the fourteenth century these suburbs vanished, presumably because of the economic recession which was a feature of that period, as well as the decline of population exacerbated by war, famine and plagues, such as the Black Death of 1349–50. The fifteenth century, if we are to judge from building work, appears to have been a period of revival, but it was only in the sixteenth century, when land became available in 1541 after the Dissolution of the Monasteries, that the town began to expand again. By the end of the sixteenth century, substantial stone dwellings, such as Rothe House, were being built (Pls 17–19).

In eastern Ireland the sixteenth century was a period of economic growth, but elsewhere it was a period of political expansion. The English government, now poised to play a European (and subsequently a world) role, viewed Ireland as an unsafe back door through which its rivals, notably the Spanish and French, could gain entry and threaten the security of England itself. Vast sums of money were expended in a policy of conquest, and by the time this was completed, in 1603, the royal treasury had been virtually bankrupted. It was not enough to conquer territory, however; colonists had to be introduced on whose loyalty the English government could rely. The method of achieving this was plantation.

PLANTATION TOWNS

The economic decline of the Anglo-Norman colony in the fourteenth century had enabled the native Irish to regain large areas of territory during the fourteenth and fifteenth centuries. In the sixteenth century, however, the Tudor desire for political stability and security produced a more intense English involvement in Ireland. In effect, the independence of the native Irish and hibernicised English had to be removed. The policy was pursued by two means, diplomacy and conquest. Diplomacy was the cheaper of the two, but its results could not always be relied upon. By contrast, the colonisation of a territory with English settlers produced a more loyal population who could be depended on in times of crisis.

In 1556 the decision was taken to shire the territory of the O'Moores and the O'Connors in Laois and Offaly. The land was confiscated, and although the colonisation was not immediately successful, it is important in so far as it initiated a process of urbanisation that continued into the seventeenth century. Town foundation did not play an important role in this plantation, but two towns were established, one at Portlaoise (named Maryborough), the other at Daingean (named Phillipstown). The conclusion of rebellion in Munster with the death of the fifteenth Earl of Desmond in 1583 was followed two years later by a scheme 'for repeopling and inhabiting the Province of Munster'. Large areas of Cork, Kerry, Limerick and Waterford were colonised, but like Laois-Offaly the plantation appears only to have been a partial success. Baltimore, Bandon, Clonakilty and Mallow in County Cork were among the towns founded in this plantation, but older centres like Lismore, Co Waterford and Tralee were also expanded.

The most important scheme, however, was the plantation of Ulster, begun in 1609. For the first time the process of plantation was deliberately linked to town foundation and the new urban network was the result of a political strategy. Politically the towns were intended to be defended settlements, containing garrisons at strategic places, while economically they would be centres of trade, providing homes for British craftworkers and merchants. Twenty-five corporate towns were envisaged in the initial plantation plan, but only sixteen were actually built. Most were developed around existing nuclei, either recently established forts or places of traditional Irish occupation, and only two were entirely new settlements. As with the other plantations, not all of the towns were successful, and by 1641 the only sizeable plantation towns were Derry, Coleraine and Strabane. Derry (renamed Londonderry) is perhaps the best example of the new plantation town, having a Renaissance-style plan consisting of a central square ('the diamond') into which the two main streets ran at right angles to one another. Located on an island in the river

Foyle, it had natural defences, but these were enhanced by the construction of a
formidable wall which survives intact to the present day.

Other early seventeenth-century plantations resulted in the foundation of
Jamestown, Co Roscommon (1622) (Fig 20), Carrick-on-Shannon, Co Leitrim,
Gorey, Co Wexford (1619), and Longford and Lanesborough in north-west
Leinster. Elsewhere in Ireland the economic prosperity of the seventeenth century
saw the expansion of old towns and the creation of new ones. In eastern Ulster, it

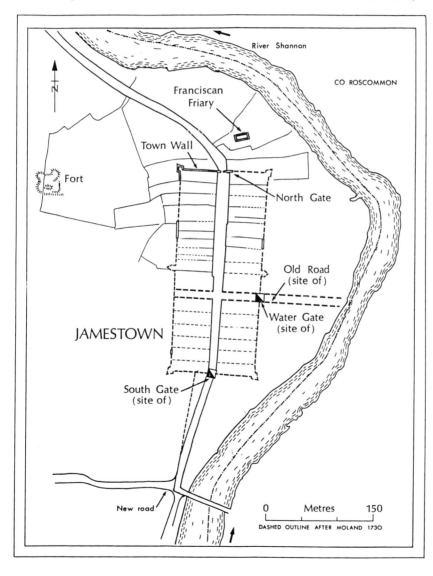

Fig 20 *Jamestown,
Co Roscommon, a
plantation town
founded in 1622 and
laid out in classic
Renaissance style.
The town walls cost
£3000 to build.*

43

was marked by the foundations at Bangor, Holywood, Killyleagh, and most importantly Belfast (1613), which was to expand into Ireland's second largest city. In the midlands, towns were established at Banagher, Ballinakill, Kilbeggan and Portarlington, while between 1670 and 1682 four towns were established in Munster, at Midleton, Charleville, Castlemartyr and Rathcormack. The most significant urban development of the seventeenth century, however, was the growth of Dublin which, by 1700, had become substantially larger than any other Irish town.

Archaeological excavations have recovered objects of seventeenth-century date in most towns, but it is only in Belfast, Carrickfergus (Fig 21), Coleraine, Derry, Dublin and Newtownards that the largescale examination of sites has occurred. At Coleraine, the site of a house on New Row, built in 1674, was examined and the house itself was removed for re-erection in the Ulster Folk Museum. Beneath the 1674 house were the stone foundations for timber-framed terrace houses, conforming to the 18 by 12 feet [5.5m x 3.6m] description given in the plantation prospectus of 1611. In Derry the remains of two rectangular early seventeenth-century houses, measuring 9m by 6m, were found in Linenhall Street. The kitchens had fine built-in ovens set in the side of the fireplaces. Storage and rubbish pits, in addition to wells, were discovered in the gardens at the rear of the houses. The intact nature of Derry's walls make it the most complete example of a fortified town in Ireland, but originally these walls were enclosed by a fosse. This has silted up, but excavation has revealed that it was 10m wide and 3m deep. Large quantities of pottery and leatherwork were recovered from the fill, and the best parallels for these artefacts are to be found in the English colonial settlements of North America. The seventeenth-century pottery from Derry and other Irish towns shows a clear change from medieval trading patterns. Pottery from Devon and the West Midlands of England predominates and continental wares are represented by German stonewares and Dutch delph. The links with France and Spain, so prominent in the medieval period, had ceased and the bulk of Ireland's trade was with Britain, a pattern that was to continue until the twentieth century.

Artillery was first used in Irish siege warfare during the late fifteenth century, but it was only in the late sixteenth and seventeenth centuries that town defences were built to withstand cannon fire. At Athlone, Co Westmeath, and Carrickfergus (Fig 21), new walls were built with protruding bastions of pentangular plan,

44

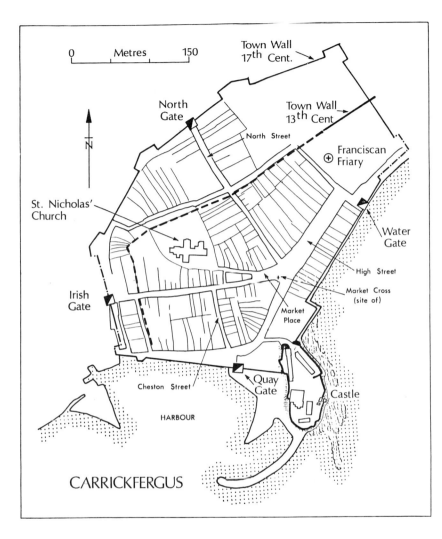

0　Metres　150

Town Wall
17th Cent.

North
Gate

Town Wall
13th Cent.

N

North Street

⊕ Franciscan
Friary

St. Nicholas'
Church

Water
Gate

High Street

Market Cross
(site of)

Irish
Gate

Market
Place

Cheston Street

Quay
Gate

Castle

HARBOUR

CARRICKFERGUS

*Fig 21 Although
founded in the
thirteenth century by
the Anglo-Normans,
Carrickfergus was
modified
considerably during
the Plantation
period. The
difference between
the course of the
medieval and
seventeenth-century
town walls is
noticeable.*

designed to accommodate the defender's guns. One of the major problems posed
by the old walls was that the stone tended to splinter when hit by cannon balls and
the fragments frequently killed or maimed the defenders. At Kilkenny, the old
medieval walls were covered during the 1640s with layers of sods and earth which

45

would absorb the cannon shot. At Ardee, an earthen artillery bastion of seventeenth-century style still survives on the town wall.

In contrast with the warfare that characterised the seventeenth century, the eighteenth century was a time of stability and prosperity for the towns. As transportation improved and business activities increased, town defences were viewed more and more as an obstacle to progress. Town gates were demolished to enable carriages and coaches to enter more easily, while the walls were knocked to make way for wider streets and housing developments as the towns began their gradual expansion into the countryside. By the end of the eighteenth century, the wheel had turned full circle. The onward march of commerce, the activity which the town walls were built to defend, had now swept them away.

GLOSSARY

Barbican: A defensive tower built outside a gate to give it added protection.

Bastion: A defensive tower usually designed to accommodate artillery and frequently of pentangular or star-shaped plan.

Earthwork: In towns, an earthen rampart often reinforced with timber and built to withstand attack.

Embrasure: In town defences, a recess built in the thickness of the wall with the purpose of accommodating archers who fired arrows through a slit or loop at the front of the embrassure.

Fosse: A defensive trench or ditch dug outside the wall or rampart.

Ringfort: A roughly circular space enclosed by an earthen bank and fosse. Ringforts are a characteristic monument type of the first millenium AD in Ireland, where they functioned primarily as habitations.

Romanesque: An architectural style based on the rounded arch which was popular throughout western Europe in the eleventh and twelfth centuries.

Souterrain ware: A type of pottery, manufactured chiefly in Ulster between the tenth and thirteenth centuries.

SELECT BIBLIOGRAPHY

Bradley, J, 'Planned Anglo-Norman towns in Ireland' in H B Clarke and A Simms (eds), *The Comparative History of Urban Origins in Non-Roman Europe* (Oxford 1985), 411–67.

'Recent archaeological research on the Irish town' in H Jäger (ed), *Stadtkernforschung* (Koln-Wien 1987), 321–70.

'The role of town plan analysis in the study of the medieval Irish town' in T R Slater (ed), *The Built Form of Western Cities* (Leicester 1990), 39–59.

Butlin, R A (ed), *The Development of the Irish Town* (London 1977).

Doherty, C, 'The monastic town in early medieval Ireland' in H B Clarke and A Simms (eds), *The Comparative History of Urban Origins in Non-Roman Europe* (Oxford 1985), 45–75.

Thomas, A, *The Walled Towns of Ireland*, 2 vols (Dublin 1992).

Wallace, P F, 'The archaeological identity of the Hiberno-Norse town', *Journal of the Royal Society of Antiquaries of Ireland,* vol 122 (1992), 35–66.

The Viking Age Buildings of Dublin, 2 vols (Dublin 1992).

INDEX

Note: Page references to illustrations are in *italics*.